Copycat Recipes

2 BOOKS IN 1: COOKBOOK TO MAKE STEP BY STEP RECIPES OF THE MOST FAMOUS RESTAURANTS IN AN EASY, FAST AND INEXPENSIVE WAY

Lina Chavez

SHORT INTRODUCTION

My name is Lina Chavez and I am very pleased to meet you.
Thank you very sincerely for purchasing my book.
In this splendid cookbook you will find the best recipes carefully selected.
OK, let us begin! Wash your hands put on an apron and start cooking.

TABLE OF CONTENTS

SHORT INTRODUCTION **3**

MAIN DISHES **7**

    CHEESE SOUFFLE..7
    OLD-FASHIONED BEEF STEW..8
    ONION SOUP (BAKED) 11
    OVEN PORCUPINES...13
    STUFFED CABBAGE ROLLS...15
    RED CABBAGE 17
    PARTY CHICKEN..18
    HAMBURGER CASSEROLE..19
    MEAT LOAF 20
    CHOW MEIN CASSEROLE 22
    POTATO AND LEEK SOUP..24
    HUNGARIAN CHICKEN PAPRIKASH 26
    AMISH MUSTARD 28
    PICKLED EGGS 29
    SOYED CHICKEN WINGS...30
    SHRIMP CREOLE 32
    ZUCCHINI BEEF SKILLET 34
    CHICKEN CURRY 36
    PENNE WITH BEEF AND GREEN PEPPERS............................38
    VEAL WITH CREAM SAUCE 39
    FRIED RICE 41
    SWEET AND SOUR SPARERIBS...42
    CHILI CON CARNE 44
    PIQUANT MEAT LOAF...46
    CAPE COD FISH CHOWDER..47
    PORK CHOPS WITH AMBER RICE...49
    LEG OF LAMB IN A CRUST 50
    SWISS STEAK 51
    LASAGNE..53
    HAMBURG STEW 55
    SCOTCH EGGS 57
    COTTAGE CHEESE PANCAKES...59
    MARZETTI CASSEROLE 61

SAUCES AND DRESSINGS **63**

    BARBECUE SAUCE..63
    CREAM SAUCE 65
    CHEESE SAUCE 66
    EGG SAUCE..67
    SAUCE FINES HERBES 67
    PARSLEY SAUCE 67

MUSHROOM SAUCE 67
TOMATO SAUCE 68
FRENCH DRESSING 68
TASTY SALAD DRESSING 70

VEGETABLES AND SALADS **71**

CUCUMBER AND TOMATOES SALAD 71
RHINELANDER SALAD 73
APPLE WALDORF 73
MANDARIN ORANGE SALAD 74
BEAN SALAD 76
HOT POTATO SALAD 77
CAULIFLOWER SALAD 79
CHICKEN & SOUR CREAM.. 81
LIMA BEAN CASSEROLE 83
PICKLED ONIONS.. 84
VEGETABLE MEDLEY 86

BREADS AND CAKES **88**

UNDERGROUND RAILROAD CORN BREAD 88
PUMPKIN BREAD 90
IRISH SODA BREAD... 92
BANANA BREAD.. 93
APPLESAUCE RAISIN BREAD....................................... 95
HONEY PINEAPPLE BREAD.. 96
POPPY SEED CAKE.. 97
DREAM CAKE... 99
STRAWBERRY WHIPPED CREAM CAKE 100
BANANA SPLIT CAKE 101
MIRACLE WHIP CHOCOLATE CAKE 103
PINEAPPLE UPSIDE-DOWN CAKE.............................. 104
PRIZE CHEESE CAKE 106
MARBLE CHIFFON CAKE 108
BLACK FOREST CAKE 110
CARROT CAKE... 112
THE WITCH'S CAKE... 114
MYSTERY BAR CAKE 115

COOKIES **116**

SWEDISH BUTTER BALLS COOKIES 116
CHERRY SNOWBALLS 118
COWBOY COOKIES 119
CUP CAKES 121
PEANUT BUTTER CHOCOLATE CHIP COOKIES 123
GERMAN CHRISTMAS COOKIES 124
HONEY COOKIES 126
SHORTBREAD 128

DATE COOKIES 130
MACAROONS DE LUSCE 131
PINEAPPLE NUT COOKIES 132
FUDGE CUTS 134
BUTTERSCOTCH COOKIES 136
PUFFED WHEAT COOKIES 137
MAPLE FUDGE 138
CHOCOLATE CHEESE COOKIES 140
DADS COCONUT COOKIES 141

PIES **142**

PECAN PIE 142
GRASSHOPPER PIE 143
RHUBARB & STRAWBERRY PIE 146

SQUARES **148**

TROPICAL PEANUT SQUARES 148
NANAIMO BARS 149
CHERRY TORTE 150
MUD HEN BARS 152
PINEAPPLE SQUARES 154
APPLE CRISP 156

DRINKS **157**

PUNCH 157
TIA MARIA 159
CHINESE GIN 159

Main Dishes

CHEESE SOUFFLE

Ingredients
1 cup milk
2 cup soft white bread crumbs, free of crusts
3 tbsp. Butter
3 tbsp. Flour
½ tsp. salt
     dash of cayenne pepper
1 cup grated nippy cheese
3 egg yolks
3 egg whites

Instructions
Pour ½ cup of milk over crumbs and let stand.
Melt butter in saucepan; blend in flour, add seasonings and
remaining ½ cup of milk. Cook over low heat, stirring constantly,
until sauce has thickened. Add cheese and stir until melted.
Remove from heat; blend soaked crumbs in the beaten egg yolks.
Cool and fold mixture into stiffly beaten egg whites. Pour into
casserole greased on bottom only. Dish should be 2/3 full. Place
in pan with inch of hot water. Oven poach in oven 350 degrees
until set, about 50 minutes. (When cooked, a silver knife inserted
into centre of soufflé will come out with no uncooked mixture
clinging to it.) Makes 6 servings. For Dinner serve with scalloped
potatoes, choice of vegetable and waldorf salad.

OLD-FASHIONED BEEF STEW

Ingredients

½ cup flour
1 tsp. salt
¼ tsp. pepper
2 lb. beef stew meat, cut into 1" pieces
2 tbsp. shortening
6 cups hot water
3 pared medium potatoes, cut in 1" cubes
1 medium turnip, cut into 1" cubes
4 carrots, cut into 1" slices
1 green pepper, cut into strips
1 cup sliced celery, cut into 1" pieces
½ cup diced onion
1 tbsp. salt
2 beef bouillon cubes
1 bay leaf

Instructions

Mix flour, 1 tsp. salt and the pepper. Coat meat with flour mixture. Melt shortening in large skillet; brown meat thoroughly.

Add water; heat to boiling. Reduce heat; cover and simmer 2 hours. Stir in remaining ingredients. Simmer 30 minutes or until vegetables are tender.

If desired, thicken stew. In covered jar, shake 1 cup cold water and 2 to 4 tbsp. Flour until blended. Stir into stew; heat to a boil, stirring constantly. Boil and stir 1 minute. (6 servings)

ONION SOUP (BAKED)

Ingredients
Onions
Beef or chicken broth
White bread
Sharp grated cheese
Use individual baking dishes

Instructions
Slice 2 large onions for each serving and cook in butter until they are done, (not brown, but shining). Place the two sliced cooked onions in each baking dish, add ½ cup of broth to each dish. Break up white bread to fill top, mounding it a bit. Add ½ cup grated sharp cheese letting it fill around and over the bread. This is very important. Bake until bubbling hot and serve at once.

OVEN PORCUPINES

Ingredients

1 lb. ground beef
½ cup uncooked regular rice
½ cup water
1/3 cup chopped onion
1 tsp. salt
½ tsp. celery salt
1/8 tsp. garlic powder
1/8 tsp. pepper
1 can (15 oz.) tomatoes sauce
1 cup water
2 tsp. Worcestershire sauce

Instructions

Heat oven to 350 degrees. Mix meat, rice, ½ cup water, the onion, salt, garlic powder and pepper. Shape mixture by rounded tablespoonfuls into balls. Place meatballs in ungreased baking dish, 8x8x2 inches. Stir together remaining ingredients; pour over meatballs. Cover with aluminum foil; bake 45 minutes. Uncover; bake 15 minutes longer. 4 to 6 servings.

STUFFED CABBAGE ROLLS

Ingredients

12 large cabbage leaves
1 ¼ lbs. beef
2 tsp. salt
¼ tsp. pepper
1 cup cooked rice
½ cup chopped onion
1 egg
½ tsp. thyme
1 (14 oz.) can tomatoes sauce
1 tbsp. sugar
1 tbsp. lemon juice
¼ cup water

Instructions

Cover cabbage leaves with boiling water for 5 minutes. Drain. Combine next 7 ingredients and ½ can sauce. Place equal portions of meat in centre of each leaf. Roll up and fasten with toothpicks. Place in large skillet. Stir in remaining sauce, sugar, lemon juice & water. Simmer covered 1 hour.

RED CABBAGE

Ingredients
1 red cabbage shredded (2 lb)
¾ cup boiling water
2 large cooking apples peeled and sliced very thin
3 tbsp. Brown sugar
1 ½ tsp. flour
1 ½ tsp. Salt
1/8 tsp. pepper
¼ cup white vinegar
3 tbsp. melted butter

Instructions
Put cabbage and water in large saucepan and cover. Boil 10 minutes, add apples and continue boiling until cabbage and apples are tender, about 10 minutes more. Do not drain. Combine brown sugar, flour, salt and pepper in a small bowl. Stir in vinegar and melted butter. Stir into cabbage and bring to a boil. Serve immediately. Serves 4-6 people.

PARTY CHICKEN

Ingredients

2-2 ½ lb. fryers, cut up, skin removed
1 ½ tsp. salt
½ tsp. pepper
½ cup corn oil margarine
1 cup white wine
1 4 oz. can mushrooms or fresh
1 large onion
4 tbsp. corn starch
½ cup water

Instructions

Season chicken, brown in melted margarine in skillet over medium heat; add chopped onion. Cover skillet and simmer until tender, about 30 minutes. Add wine and simmer 10 minutes. Add mushrooms, heat through. Blend corn starch and water and add to skillet. Boil 1 minute. Serve with rice and broccoli.

HAMBURGER CASSEROLE (SLOW COOKER)

Ingredients
2 large finely sliced potatoes
3 medium carrots sliced
1 #2 can peas, well drained
3 medium onions sliced
1 ½ lbs. lean ground beef browned
2 stalks celery, sliced
1 ten oz. can tomato soup
1 ten oz. can water

Instructions
Place layers of vegetables in the order given, in the slow cooker. Season each layer with salt and pepper. Put the beef on top of celery. Mix tomatoes with water and pour into slow cooker. Cover and set to low for 6 to 8 hours or set to high for 2 to 4 hours. This recipe may be used to cook in dutch oven at 350 degrees for 45 to 55 minutes. Serves 8.

MEAT LOAF

Ingredients

3 cups ground beef (1/2 pork & ½ beef is also good)
1 or 2 eggs
1 tsp. chopped parsley (dried is okay)
2 good sized onions
1 cup bread crumbs
1 cup milk
1 tsp. salt
  Pepper
2 tsp. Bacon drippings
2 tsp. Catsup
½ diced green pepper

Instructions

Mix all ingredients thoroughly except milk and egg. Beat egg thoroughly and add milk. Add egg, milk mixture to meat. Press into greased loaf pan, put 2 or 3 strips of bacon over top and bake in 350 degree oven 30 to 40 minutes until done.

CHOW MEIN CASSEROLE

Ingredients

1 10 oz. can cream of mushroom soup
1 7 oz. can tuna
1 can chow mein noodles
½ cup chopped celery
½ cup chopped onions
1 10 oz. can mushrooms (drain ½ liquid)
   Salt & pepper to taste

Instructions

Heat soup. Put in onions and celery and let simmer 10 minutes. Put in other ingredients, keeping out enough noodles to sprinkle over top. Place in casserole and bake at 350 degrees for 25 minutes. Serves 3-4.

POTATO AND LEEK SOUP

<u>Ingredients</u>
¼ cup butter
4 leeks (white part only) finely chopped
½ cup finely chopped green onions
4 large potatoes, diced (4 cups)
4 cups water
3 tsp. salt
½ tsp. pepper
3 cups milk, scalded
1 tbsp. butter

<u>Instructions</u>
Melt ¼ cup butter in large saucepan and add leeks and onions.
Cook gently, stirring, 5 minutes. Do not brown. Add potatoes,
water, salt and pepper. Cover and cook over moderate heat
about 30 minutes or until vegetables are tender. Rub mixture
through a sieve or whirl in a blender. Return to saucepan.
Bring back to a boil and stir in hot milk and 1 tbsp. butter.
Taste and add more salt if necessary.

HUNGARIAN CHICKEN PAPRIKASH

Ingredients

1 3 lb. chicken, salt & pepper
3 tbsp. shortening
2 medium onions minced
1 tbsp. paprika
1 cup water
1 cup sour cream
½ cup flour

Instructions

Salt and pepper chicken pieces, sauté in shortening until golden, add onions and continue sauté for 30 minutes. Remove from heat, stir in paprika. Then add water and return to heat. Simmer gently for about 15 minutes adding a little more water if needed. Shake the pan gently from time to time instead of stirring. Before serving, mix sour cream and flour with enough water to make a smooth paste; and slowly to chicken, blend well. Simmer for a few minutes. Ready to serve.

AMISH MUSTARD

<u>Ingredients</u>
¾ cup white vinegar
3 tbsp. Flour
2 tbsp. Dry mustard
  pinch of salt
1 egg
1 cup of vinegar
1 cup of milk
2 tbsp. Of butter approximately turmeric for coloring

<u>Instructions</u>
Add vinegar after all the other ingredients have cooked, then cook some more.

PICKLED EGGS

<u>Ingredients</u>
3 cups white vinegar
1 ½ cups water
1 ½ tsp. salt
1 tsp. whole cloves
1 tsp. pepper corns
½ tsp. celery salt or seed
12 eggs

<u>Instructions</u>
Combine: vinegar, water, salt, cloves, pepper corns and celery salt in a saucepan. Boil 10 minutes. Strain and cool.
Put eggs in large pan, cover with cold water. Set on heat and bring water to full boil.
Cover pan and remove from heat and let eggs stand 20 minutes. Run cold water over eggs until they are cold then shell. Pack into jars, pour vinegar mix over eggs in jars. Cover and refrigerate. Let stand at least 2 days before using.

SOYED CHICKEN WINGS

Ingredients

1 ½ lbs. chicken wings (about 7)
¼ tsp. ground ginger
½ tsp. dry mustard
1 tbsp. olive oil
3 tbsp. soy sauce
   Juice of ½ lemon

Instructions

Put chicken wings in large plastic bag. Combine remaining ingredients, pour into plastic bag, toss and refrigerate 1 hour or longer. Arrange one layer deep in shallow pan and bake in preheated 425 degree oven, turning once, 35 minutes or until wings are very tender.

SHRIMP CREOLE

Ingredients

3 lbs. fresh or frozen shrimp
1 medium onion, chopped
1 clove garlic, finely chopped
1 green pepper, chopped
2 stalks celery chopped
1 tbsp. shortening
1 ½ cups canned tomatoes
1 cup tomatoes sauce
1 tsp. thyme
1 bay leaf
1 tbsp. chopped parsley
½ tbsp. sugar
   salt, pepper to taste
   boiled rice

Instructions

Boil shrimp approximately 10 minutes, peel clean. Sauté next four ingredients in melted shortening. Simmer 5 minutes, add remaining ingredients except rice, add shrimp. Simmer ½ hour. Serve in circle of boiled rice. Serves 6.

ZUCCHINI BEEF SKILLET

Ingredients

1 lb. ground round steak
1 small onion, chopped
1 19 oz. can tomatoes or
  14 oz. can tomato sauce
1 cup chopped dill pickle
1 clove garlic, chopped or
  garlic powder
¾ tsp. salt
  dash of pepper
¾ lb. zucchini or other summer squash, sliced

Instructions

In large skillet brown beef with onion over medium heat; stirring frequently. Add tomatoes, dill pickle, garlic, salt and pepper. Simmer uncovered 5 minutes. Mix in zucchini, cover and cook 15 minutes longer or until zucchini is tender.

CHICKEN CURRY

Ingredients

1 broiler-fryer (2 ½ to 3 lbs) cut up
2 tsp. salt
2 tbsp. vegetable oil
1 onion, chopped
2 cloves garlic, crushed
1 can (5 ½ oz.) tomato paste
1 cup water
1 ½ tbsp. curry powder
1 tsp. sugar
½ pint sour cream

Instructions

Sprinkle chicken with salt; in skillet brown chicken in oil. Add onion and garlic; cook until onion is very soft. Pour off fat. Combine tomato paste, water, curry powder and sugar; pour over chicken. Simmer, covered 35 minutes to 40 minutes or until chicken is tender. Remove skillet from heat and blend in sour cream. Over very low heat warm through but do not allow to boil. Serve over rice. Serves 4 to 6 persons.

PENNE WITH BEEF AND GREEN PEPPERS

Ingredients
1 lb. ground beef
1 cup diced green pepper
1/3 cup chopped onion
2 tbsp. vegetable oil
½ cup dry white wine or beef broth
    28 oz. can tomatoes
1 tsp. salt
¼ tsp. pepper
    16 oz. penne

Instructions
In large saucepan, sauté beef, green pepper and onion in
vegetable oil. Stir frequently until meat is browned. Add wine
and simmer 10 minutes. Add tomatoes, salt and pepper.
Simmer 40-45 minutes.
Prepare penne in large amount of boiling salted water as
package directs. Drain. Pour prepared sauce over cooked
penne arranged in serving dish. Serves 6-8.

VEAL WITH CREAM SAUCE

Ingredients

2 lbs. veal, trimmed
3 tbsp. vegetable oil
¼ tsp. crushed peppercorns
¼ tsp. caraway seeds, crushed
1 tbsp. butter
1 large onion, diced
½ lb. mushrooms
2 cups white wine
1 pint 35% cream

Instructions

Cut veal in thin slices about 1" in diameter. Sauté quickly in vegetable oil, add salt, pepper and caraway seeds.
Remove meat, add butter and onions and fry lightly. Add mushrooms, white wine and cream, reduce to half. Season and pour over meat. Serves 4-5.

FRIED RICE

<u>Ingredients</u>
2 tbsp. chopped onion
½ cup mushroom stems and pieces
½ cup finely chopped cooked chicken, pork or ham
2 tbsp. cooking oil
4 cups cold cooked rice
2 tbsp. soy sauce
1 egg, well beaten
2 tbsp. minced parsley
1/8 tsp. pepper

<u>Instructions</u>
Sauté onion, mushrooms and chicken in oil in large skillet until tender. Add rice and soy sauce. Cook over low heat 5 to 10 minutes stirring occasionally with a fork. Add egg, parley and pepper. Cook over low heat 5 minutes stirring constantly with a fork. If desired, add additional soy sauce.

SWEET AND SOUR SPARERIBS

Ingredients

2 ¼ cups catsup
2 ½ tbsp. worcestershire sauce
¾ tsp. cayenne pepper
¾ tsp. chili powder
½ cup vinegar
1 cup salt pork liquor
1 cup sugar
6-8 cloves garlic
2 medium onions chopped
¼ cup chopped sweet pickle mixture
1 ½ lbs. spareribs

Instructions

Combine all ingredients in saucepan on slow simmer. Brown spareribs in fry pan and put in sauce to simmer until cooked. NOTE: salt pork is made by boiling 2 strips salt pork in 1 ½ cups water for about 5 minutes. Drain off 1 cup liquor.

CHILI CON CARNE

<u>Ingredients</u>

2 lbs. ground beef
2 medium onions
  Salt
  Pepper
  Flavor salt
  Garlic salt
1 small can tomatoes sauce
1 can tomatoes soup + ½ can water
2 cans of mushrooms (juice and all)
1 can red kidney beans
  Chili powder to suite taste

<u>Instructions</u>

Fry onions in bacon drippings to brown slightly, add meat and season to taste. Cook until meat is slightly browned. Add rest of ingredients and cook together about ½ hour or until thickened.
Serve with crusty rolls.

PIQUANT MEAT LOAF

Ingredients
2/3 cup bread crumbs
1 cup milk
1 ½ lbs. ground beef
2 eggs slightly beaten
1 tsp. salt
1 large onion
1/8 tsp. pepper
½ or less tsp. sage
3 tbsp. brown sugar
3 tbsp. catsup
¼ tsp. nutmeg
1 tsp. dry mustard

Instructions
Soak crumbs in milk. Add beef, eggs, onion and seasoning.
Pack lightly. Combine brown sugar, catsup, nutmeg and dry
mustard. Spread over unbaked loaf.
Bake in 350 degree oven for 1 ¼ hours. Serves 6-8.

CAPE COD FISH CHOWDER

Ingredients

1/3 cup chopped onion
1 ½ tbsp. butter or margarine
1 large potato (1-1/3 cup) (cubed)
½ tsp. salt
¼ tsp. basil
    Pinch pepper
1 ¼ cups water
½ lb. frozen cod or haddock, partly thawed & cubed.
1 can (8 oz.) whole kernel corn
1 small can evaporated milk (2/3 cup)

Instructions

Sauté onion in butter, add potatoes, salt, basil, pepper and water. Cover. Simmer 15 minutes. Stir in corn and liquid and milk. Cover.
Heat to a boil.

PORK CHOPS WITH AMBER RICE

Ingredients
6   pork chops ¾ inch thick
    Salt and pepper
1 1/3 cups packaged precooked 8minute rice) rice
1   cup orange juice
1   can condensed chicken rice soup

Instructions
Brown pork chops in heavy skillet; season with salt and
pepper. Place rice in 12" x 10" x 2" baking dish; pour orange
juice over rice, arrange browned pork chops on rice. Pour
chicken soup over all. Cover and bake in moderate oven 350
degrees for 45 minutes. Uncover and bake 10 minutes longer.
Makes 6 servings. Salad, rolls etc.

LEG OF LAMB IN A CRUST

Ingredients

1 4-5 lb. leg of lamb, boned
1 lamb kidney, diced (or giblets)
¼ lb. mushrooms, sliced
2 tbsp. butter
2 tbsp. Madeira
½ tsp. thyme
½ tsp. rosemary
½ tsp. tarragon
1 tbsp. butter
2 cups puff pastry or regular pie
1 egg yolk

Instructions

Brown kidney and mushrooms in butter. Deglaze pan with maderia and add seasoning to taste. Fill cavities in leg of lamb and stitch or secure with meat skewer. Rub lightly with butter and cook in 350 degree oven for 2 hours or to desired doneness. Remove from oven, remove skewer and wrap in thinly rolled pastry. Glaze pastry surface with egg yolk. Bake in 425 degree oven for 15-20 minutes.

SWISS STEAK

Ingredients

2 or 3 steaks, cut from short rib roast
2 tbsp. flour
1 tsp. salt
1/8 tsp. pepper
2 tbsp. oil
1 20 oz. can stewed tomatoes
¼ cup chopped onion
1 tsp. dry mustard
½ tsp. chili powder
2 tsp. worcestershire sauce
1 tsp. sugar
¼ cup water
1 small bay leaf

Instructions

Combine flour, salt and pepper and pound into meat, using a meat pounder. Heat oil in a heavy saucepan and brown meat on both sides. Combine remaining ingredients and pour over steaks. Cover and cook slowly until tender – 1 ½ to 2 hours. Add more water if needed during cooking. Skim off excess fat.

LASAGNE

Ingredients

1 medium onion (½ cup) finely chopped
1 clove garlic (1 tsp. garlic salt)
2 tbsp. olive oil
1 lb. ground beef
4 oz. can tomato paste
14 oz. can tomatoes sauce
2 tsp. salt
1 tsp. oregano
1 egg
   16 oz. cottage cheese (creamed)
1 small package cream cheese
1/3 cup grated parmesan cheese
6-8 lasagne noodles
1 package (6oz.) sliced mozzarella cheese

Instructions

Sauté onion and garlic in 1 tablespoon olive oil.
Add ground beef and brown. Blend in tomatoes sauce,
tomato paste, 1 tsp. salt and oregano. Simmer 15 minutes. Mix
cottage cheese, cream cheese, parmesan cheese, egg, olive oil
and salt.
Pour half meat sauce in oblong pan 9 x 13 and cover with
layer of half of lasagna noodles. Spread all cottage cheese
mixture over lasagne; cover with remaining lasagna noodles.
Top with remaining sauce. Arrange strips of mozzarella
cheese on top. Bake in 350 degree oven for 25-30 minutes.
Serve hot.

HAMBURG STEW

Ingredients

1 ½ lbs. ground beef or beef pork mixed
2 medium onions
4 medium carrots
4 medium potatoes

Instructions

Fry chopped onions in bacon drippings slightly in dutch oven
or frying pan. Add the ground meat and season well with salt,
pepper, seasoned salt or garlic salt and cook about 10-15
minutes until slightly browned. Add water to cover and sliced
carrots and potatoes (sliced thickly). Cook about ½ hour until
vegetables are done, then thicken gravy mixed with cold
water.

SCOTCH EGGS

Ingredients
8 eggs
1 lb. sausage meat

Coating:
breadcrumbs
beaten egg

Instructions
Hard boil eggs, let cool and shell. Mould the sausage meat around the egg. Roll on a lightly floured board and form into neat shape. Dip in beaten egg, then in breadcrumbs. Fry in deep fat till golden brown. (5-7 minutes) Drain well.

COTTAGE CHEESE PANCAKES

Ingredients
1 cup creamed cottage cheese
3 eggs
3 tbsp. honey or brown sugar
  Juice of 1 lemon
½ cup flour

Instructions
Combine cheese, egg, honey, lemon juice and blend well.
Add flour, blend well.
On oiled skilled fry a tablespoon at a time until golden brown.

MARZETTI CASSEROLE

Ingredients

1 lb. ground beef
1 tsp. salt
1 can mushroom soup
¼ lb. cheese, shredded
1 small package noodles, cooked

Instructions

Brown meat, mix all ingredients together and place in casserole.
Bake in 375 degree oven for 30 minutes.

Sauces and Dressings

BARBECUE SAUCE

Ingredients

½ tsp. mustard (prepared)
1 cup ketchup
½ cup water
4 tbsp. lemon juice
2 tbsp. vinegar
2 tbsp. (heaping) brown sugar
   Diced onions & celery to taste

Instructions

Mix all ingredients together well.
Simmer for 30 minutes before brushing on meat.
This can be used with all meats, and oven baking also.
For oriental flavor, add garlic powder & drained pineapple.
For a hot sauce, add a sprinkle of cayenne.

CREAM SAUCE

Ingredients
In a sauce pan, melt
2 tbsp. butter or margarine
Blend until smooth
2 tbsp. cake & pastry flour
½ tbsp. salt
 pinch of pepper
Gradually blend in
1 cup milk

Instructions
Cook over medium heat, stirring constantly, until thickened.
Season to taste. Yield 1 cup.

CHEESE SAUCE

Instructions
Prepare cream sauce and stir in:
¾ cup grated cheddar cheese.
Heat until smoothly blended.

EGG SAUCE

Prepare cream sauce and stir in:
1 hard cooked egg, chopped.
Serve with fish, vegetables or croquettes.

SAUCE FINES HERBES

Prepare cream sauce and stir in:
¼ cup finely chopped fresh herbs.
    (chives, tarragon, chervil, green onions, dill).

PARSLEY SAUCE

Prepare cream sauce and stir in:
¼ cup chopped parsley.

MUSHROOM SAUCE

Prepare cream sauce and stir in:
½ cup chopped or sliced cooked mushrooms.

TOMATO SAUCE

Prepare cream sauce and stir in:
1 tbsp. tomato puree or
2 tbsp. tomato sauce.

FRENCH DRESSING

Ingredients
1 tin tomato soup
1 cup sunflower oil
¾ cup white vinegar
1 cup sugar
1 tbsp. prepared mustard
1 tbsp. Worcestershire sauce
1 tsp. salt
1 tsp. onion juice
1 tsp. garlic juice
¼ tsp. pepper

Instructions
Blend together.

TASTY SALAD DRESSING

Ingredients
1 egg (beaten)
1 tbsp. sugar
4 tbsp. vinegar or pickle juice
1 tsp. salt
1 tsp. pepper
1 tsp. mustard
1 tsp. butter

Instructions
Cook until thickened in double boiler.
Add milk or cream to thin for use.

Vegetables and Salads

CUCUMBER AND TOMATOES SALAD

Ingredients
4 cucumbers
1 tbsp. salt
2 tbsp. wine vinegar
5 tbsp. olive oil
1 tbsp. chopped parsley
   Freshly ground pepper
2 tomatoes quartered
1 hard-cooked egg, sliced

Instructions
Cut cucumbers, remove seeds, slice in sections.
Place in salad bowl, sprinkle with salt, mix well, keep chilled
for 2 hours. Drain, wash with cold water, drain again.
Add next 4 ingredients and toss gently.
Place in salad bowl and garnish with tomatoes sections and
egg slices.

RHINELANDER SALAD

Ingredients
1 cup sugar
¼ cup vinegar
2 cup well drained sauerkraut
1 cup chopped celery
1 cup chopped onion
2/3 cup chopped red pepper (optional)

Instructions
Boil vinegar and sugar 1 minute.
Cool and pour over vegetables. Let stand overnight in refrigerator.
This is a good barbecue salad.

APPLE WALDORF

Serve on lettuce leaves.
Toss three cups of diced apples, one cup of thinly sliced celery and a quarter cup of chopped walnuts, with enough miracle whip to moisten.
Serve garnished with miracle whip on top.

MANDARIN ORANGE SALAD

Ingredients

2 packages of commercial sour cream
2 cups tiny marshmallows
½ package angel shred cocoanut
1 tin pineapple chunks
2 small tins of mandarin oranges

Instructions

Blend these ingredients & leave at room temp.
This helps to dissolve marshmallows into dressing.
Then add pineapple & mandarin oranges, well drained.
Chill & it should stand a few hours before serving.

BEAN SALAD

<u>Ingredients</u>
1 tin yellow & green beans
1 tin lima & kidney beans
2 medium onions sliced thin
½ cup green pepper chopped lightly
¾ cup white sugar
2/3 cup white vinegar
½ cup salad oil
    Salt & pepper

<u>Instructions</u>
Mix well, pour over vegetables. Marinate overnight drain and serve.

HOT POTATO SALAD

Ingredients

8 medium size potatoes
12 slices cooked bacon (diced & reserve drippings)
3 medium size onions (diced)
¾ cup white vinegar
2 ½ tbsp. sugar
2 tsp. salt
¾ tsp. accent
¼ tsp. freshly ground pepper

Instructions

Simmer onions in bacon drippings until transparent. Stir in mixture of vinegar, sugar, salt, accent, pepper & diced bacon. Heat to boiling. Pour over potatoes, keep in moderate oven until ready to serve.

CAULIFLOWER SALAD

Ingredients

1 med. size cauliflower
1 5 oz. can shrimp
¼ cup white vinegar
3 tbsp. salad oil
½ tsp. salt
1/8 tsp. white pepper
¼ tsp. oregano
    Chopped onion

Instructions

Clean & separate cauliflower into florets.
Wash & drain shrimp. Chill in separate bowls.
Combine remaining ingredients & shake well. Toss over
mixed shrimp & cauliflower, chill again & serve.

CHICKEN & SOUR CREAM

Ingredients

4 chicken breasts
4 tbsp. butter (add more if needed)
¼ tsp. salt
¾ tsp. accent
1 bay leaf
1 small carton sour cream

Instructions

Bake chicken in oven ¾ hr. at 300 degrees, in the butter.
Remove and place on stove at medium heat, adding more butter if required.
Add onions, bay leaf, salt & accent. Simmer 15 minutes.
Remove chicken, add a little flour and stir until smooth.
Add sour cream and stir until well blended. Do not boil. Pour over chicken and sprinkle with a little paprika and parsley.

LIMA BEAN CASSEROLE

Ingredients
1 pkg. dry lima beans (cooked)
1 qt. canned tomatoes
1 bay leaf
1 cup onion chopped
1 cup celery chopped
1 clove garlic
   Salt and pepper
1 lb. pork sausage (browned)

Instructions
Combine first seven ingredients. Arrange sausages on top.
Bake slow 2 to 3 hours, in 300 degree oven.

PICKLED ONIONS

Ingredients

1 10 lb. bag of silver skin onions
½ gal. white vinegar
4 tbsp. salt
½ cup mixed pickling spice
4 tbsp. white sugar

Instructions

Peel onions, put in crock with 2 to 3 cups of coarse salt and boiling water. Let stand overnight. Drain in the morning. Boil together, pour over pickles and let sit. Add 3 lb. white sugar for 2 to 3 days a few handfuls at a time.
Stir daily until dissolved. Bottle or leave in crock.

VEGETABLE MEDLEY

Ingredients

¼ lb. green pepper
½ lb. eggplant
½ lb. zucchini
4-5 tomatoes (fresh)
¾ cup chopped onion
1 tbsp. chopped garlic
1 cup olive oil
1 tsp. salt
½ tsp. pepper
2 bay leaves
¼ tsp. thyme
¼ tsp. basil

Instructions

Cut green pepper, eggplant, zucchini, tomatoes in 1" square cubes. Sauté onion & garlic in oil & simmer 2-3 minutes. Add remaining ingredients, simmer 20-25 minutes or until vegetables are tender. Hot or cold appetizer. Serves 4.

Breads and Cakes

UNDERGROUND RAILROAD CORN BREAD

Ingredients

1 ½ lbs. (6 cups) flour

1 cup sugar

1 ½ lbs. (4 ½ cups) corn meal

1 oz. (2 2/3 tbsp) baking powder

1 tsp. salt

4 eggs

1 cup cooking oil

1 quart buttermilk

1 quart homogenized milk

1 pint water

Instructions

Bake at 375 degrees for 20-30 minutes.

PUMPKIN BREAD

<u>Ingredients</u>
3 cup sugar
1 cup salad oil
4 eggs (add 1 at a time)
2 tsp. nutmeg
1 tbsp. cinnamon
2/3 cup water
1 ¾ cup pumpkin (1 ¾ cup)
3 ½ cup flour
2 tsp. baking soda

<u>Instructions</u>
Fill pans ½ full. Bake at 325 degrees for 1 hour & 15 minutes, or until done when tested.

IRISH SODA BREAD

Ingredients

4 cups sifted all purpose. Flour
1 tsp. salt
3 tsp. baking powder
1 tsp. soda
¼ cup sugar (optional)
¼ cup butter or margarine
1 egg
1 ¾ cups butter milk

Instructions
Knead until smooth 2 or 3 minutes.
Bake 35 to 40 minutes at 375 degrees.

BANANA BREAD

Ingredients

½ cup butter
1 cup sugar
2 eggs
2 cups flour
1 tsp. soda
3 bananas (crushed)
¼ cup chopped nuts

Instructions

Cream butter, sugar, add beaten eggs, flour and soda. Crush bananas & mix. Add nuts.

Place in a greased bread pan & bake in a moderate hot oven 45-60 minutes. (350-375 degrees).

APPLESAUCE RAISIN BREAD

<u>Ingredients</u>
1 egg (slightly beaten)
1 cup applesauce
¼ cup melted butter or margarine
½ cup granulated sugar
¼ cup brown sugar (firmly packed)
2 cups sifted all purpose flour
2 tsp. baking powder
¾ tsp. salt
½ tsp. soda
½ tsp. cinnamon
1 tsp. nutmeg
½ cup seedless raisins
1 cup coarsely chopped pecans or walnuts

<u>Instructions</u>
In a bowl combine egg, applesauce, melted butter, sugars, blending well. Stir in the flour, baking powder, salt, soda, and spices. Stir until smooth. Add nuts.
Put into well greased 5 by 9 loaf pan.
350 degree oven for about one hour.

HONEY PINEAPPLE BREAD

<u>Ingredients</u>
2 tbsp. Salad oil
1 cup honey
1 egg, slightly beaten
2 cups sifted regular all-purpose flour
2 tsp. baking powder
¾ tsp. salt
1 cup whole bran
1 cup pineapple juice
¾ cup chopped walnuts

<u>Instructions</u>
In a bowl blend well, oil honey egg.
Stir in flour, baking powder, salt, whole bran and pineapple juice, mixing just until dry ingredients are moistened.
Fold in nuts. Pour into greased 5" x 9" bread loaf pan and bake in 350 degree oven for 1 hour. Makes 1 loaf.

POPPY SEED CAKE

Ingredients

3 eggs
2 cups white sugar
1 ¼ cup cooking oil
½ cup poppy seeds
3 cups five roses flour
3 tsp. baking powder
½ tsp. baking soda
1/8 tsp. salt
1 large tin carnation milk

Instructions

Bake 1 hour at 300 degrees.
Do not use pastry flour. Will make 3 loaf pans or 1 large 12 x 8 x 2".

DREAM CAKE

<u>Ingredients</u>
2 eggs
1 cup sugar
2 cups flour
2 tsp. baking powder
1 cup melted butter or margarine

<u>Instructions</u>
Whip eggs lightly, add sugar and whip for 5 minutes. Add baking powder to flour. The flour and melted butter are then added alternately in small portions to egg mixture. Pour into cake form and bake for 45-55 minutes in a warm oven 350 degrees.

<u>Icing</u>
3-4 bananas
Juice of 1 orange
3 tbsp. sugar
3 tbsp. rum
Grated orange peel
1 cup chopped nuts

Mix orange juice, rum and sugar. Whip the cream and add some rum mixture. Edge cake with cream sprinkle nuts. Slice bananas on top of cake then pour rest of rum mixture on top soaking cake. Decorate with orange rind.

STRAWBERRY WHIPPED CREAM CAKE

Ingredients
2 ½ cups sugar
1 tsp. salt
3 cups egg yolks
¼ cup egg whites
2 cups cake flour
1 tsp. baking powder
1 cup milk
½ cup butter
½ tsp. vanilla

Instructions
Whip first four ingredients at medium speed for 25 minutes or until the batter peaks and falls slowly. Sift flour and baking powder twice. Melt butter into milk and add vanilla. Fold alternately flour mixture and milk mixture into sugar-yolk mixture. Blend well, do not whip. Pour batter into three greased 8 inch round cake pans. Bake in 370 degree oven until golden brown. 15-20 minutes.

Topping
1 quart whipping cream whipped
1 oz. cherry brandy
2 cups chopped and sugared strawberries

Add cherry brandy to cream. Put strawberries into ½ of the whipped cream and spread cream mixture between 3 cake layers. Cover the cake with the remaining whipped cream and decorate with whole strawberries. Refrigerate before serving.

BANANA SPLIT CAKE

Ingredients
1 cup graham cracker crumbs
1 stick margarine

Instructions
Mix together and press in pan and bake at 350 degrees for 5 minutes.

Topping
1 stick margarine
1 cup icing sugar
1 egg
½ tsp. vanilla

Beat for 20 minutes no less. Spread over graham crackers, top with 2 bananas (sliced) 1-14 oz. tin crushed pineapple well drained over bananas. Top with one envelope dream whip (beaten). Sprinkle with nuts and cherries.
Set in refrigerator for several hours to set.

MIRACLE WHIP CHOCOLATE CAKE

Ingredients
2 cups flour
1 cup white sugar
2 tsp. baking soda
3 tbsp. Cocoa
1 cup miracle whip
1 cup lukewarm water
1 tsp. vanilla

Instructions
Sift all dry ingredients together and add all at one to the liquid ingredients, just beat enough to blend. Pour into 8 inch cake pan, bake in 350 degree oven 45 to 55 minutes.

PINEAPPLE UPSIDE-DOWN CAKE

Ingredients
¼ cup butter or margarine
½ cup brown sugar (packed)
1 can (8 ½ ounces) pineapple
   Slices, drained and cut into halves
Maraschino cherries
Pecan halves
1 pkg. yellow cake mix

Instructions
Heat oven to 350 degrees. Melt butter over low heat in layer pan, 9 x 1 ½ inch pan. Sprinkle brown sugar evenly over butter.

Arrange pineapple halves, cherries and pecans over sugar mixture. Prepare cake mix as directed on package. Pour half the batter (about 2 ½ cups) evenly over fruit in pan. Bake 35 to 45 minutes or until wooden pick inserted in centre comes out clean. Invert at once onto serving plate. Leave pan over cake a few minutes. Serve warm plain or with whipped cream. Nine servings.

PRIZE CHEESE CAKE

Ingredients
Mix in order:
1 lb. cottage cheese
1 lb. cream cheese (2 large pkgs.)
1 ½ cups of sugar

Instructions
Beat well with mixer and add juice of lemon plus 1 teaspoon vanilla.
Sift together:
3 tbsp. Cornstarch
3 tbsp. Flour

Add this to cottage cheese mixture. Add one pint of sour cream plus ¼ lb. melted butter. Pour this mixture into graham cracker crumbs pie crust and bake for 1 hour at 325 degrees. After one hour shut off oven and leave cake in two more hours to set. After cake is completely cooled, cherry pie filling may be added on top. Pan size: 13 x 9 inch pan.

MARBLE CHIFFON CAKE

Ingredients
2 ¼ cups sifted cake flour
1 ½ cups sugar
3 tsp. baking powder
1 tsp. salt
½ cup salad oil
7 egg yolks
¾ cup cold water
1 tsp. vanilla
½ tsp. cream of tartar

Instructions
Sift dry ingredients together into bowl. Make well in centre of dry ingredients and in order salad oil, egg yolks, cold water and vanilla. Beat until satin smooth. In large bowl, beat 7 egg whites with cream of tartar until very stiff peaks form. Pour egg yolk mixture in thin stream over entire surface of egg whites, gently folding to blend. Remove 1/3 of batter to separate bowl.

Blend together ¼ cup boiling water, 2 tablespoons sugar and 2 one oz. squares unsweetened chocolate, melted cool. Gently fold chocolate mixture into 1/3 portion of batter.

Spoon half the light batter into ungreased 10 inch tube pan, top with half the chocolate batter. Repeat layers, with narrow spatula, swirl gently through batters to marble. Leave definite areas of light and dark batter.

Bake in slow oven 325 degrees about 65 minutes or until cake tests done. Invert cake in pan, cool.

Frost with chocolate frosting.

BLACK FOREST CAKE

Ingredients
5 eggs
¾ cup sugar
½ cup cocoa powder
1 cup all purpose flour
13/4 cups drained red pitted cherries

Instructions
Beat eggs and sugar until creamy stiff. Carefully add sifted cocoa and flour, pour into greased and floured 8 inch round cake pan. Bake in 350 degree oven for 15-20 minutes. When cold cut cake into 3 layers, place 1 layer on a large plate, top with drained cherries.

Garnish
1 quart whipping cream, whipped
2 oz. kirschwasser
2 oz. sugar syrup
2 cups shaved bitter sweet chocolate

Add ½ tablespoon kirschwasser to whipped cream, spread ½ inch evenly over cherries. Place on next cake layer, soak with the syrup and kirschwasser again spread ½ inch whipped cream evenly over top. Add top layer of cake.
Spread top and sides with whipped cream, sprinkly shaved chocolate over all. Garnish with rosettes of whipped cream and maraschino cherries. Serves 10.

CARROT CAKE

Ingredients
- 2 cups sifted all purpose flour
- 2 tsp. baking powder
- 2 tsp. baking soda
- 1 tsp. salt
- 3 tsp. cinnamon
- Pinch of nutmeg
- 1 cup st. lawrance corn oil
- 2 cups sugar
- 4 eggs

Instructions
Add sugar gradually to oil, beat well after each addition with electric mixer. Beat eggs separately and beat into mixture. Gradually stir in dry ingredients (do not use mixer) really thick. Add 3 cups grated raw carrots and nuts.
Grease and flour loaf pan good. Bake at 325 degrees for 60-65 minutes.

Carrot cake icing
- 1 80 oz. pkg. philadelphia cream cheese
- 3 tbsp. corn oil
- 31/2 cups sifted icing sugar
- ¼ tsp. salt

THE WITCH'S CAKE

Ingredients
10 oz. skim milk cottage cheese
4 tbsp. fine sugar
3 egg yolks
5 tbsp. strega liquor or (sweet liqueur)
4 tbsp. grated bitter chocolate
1 sponge cake 8-9 inches round
½ cup water
1 cup whipping cream, whipped
   cinnamon

Instructions
Toss cheese and sugar together, add egg yolks, toss to make the mixture foam. Divide mixture in half, add 3 tablespoons of strega and chocolate to one half. Cut cake in half, place one half on plate and cover with mixture of water and 2 tablespoons strega. Spread with white mixture then chocolate.
Cover with second cake half, refrigerate, ice with whipped cream. Sprinkle with cinnamon. Serves 8.

MYSTERY BAR CAKE

Ingredients
Bottom layer
1 cup flour
½ cup butter
2 tbsp. sugar white

Topping
2 eggs
1 tsp. baking powder
1 cup raisins
Pinch salt
1 cup brown sugar

Instructions
Mix ingredients for the bottom layer as for pastry, put in pan 8 x 8 or 9 x 9 inch pan, if desired. Bake in a moderate oven 375 for 5 minutes. Beat eggs and add remaining ingredients to make topping.
Pour over partially cooked crust, and bake at 400 degrees for 25 minutes.

Cookies

SWEDISH BUTTER BALLS COOKIES

Ingredients
1 cup soft butter
½ cup icing sugar
1 tsp. vanilla
1 cup finely chopped walnuts or pecans
2 cups flour
¼ tsp. salt

Instructions
Cream butter, sugar and vanilla. Blend in flour, salt and nuts. Mix with hands. Shape into 1 inch balls and bake at 350 degrees for 10-12 minutes. When done and balls are still hot roll in icing sugar.
Yield about 35 cookies. (Do not grease cookie sheet).

CHERRY SNOWBALLS

<u>Ingredients</u>
1 cup butter
¼ cup icing sugar
2 cups sifted all-purpose flour
½ tsp. salt
1 cup red candied cherries
1 cup finely crushed almond

<u>Instructions</u>
Cream butter and sugar until fluffy. Add remaining ingredients
except cherries. Flatten a small amount of dough about a
teaspoonful for each cookie in palm of hand.
Place a cherry on circle of dough. Cover cherry by pinching
dough up and around it, roll between palm of hand to smooth.
Bake in moderate oven 325 degrees. While still hot roll in fine
granulated fruit sugar. Makes three dozen.

COWBOY COOKIES

Ingredients

2 cups sifted flour
1 tsp. soda
½ tsp. baking powder
½ tsp. salt
1 cup shortening (margarine or butter)
½ pkg. semi-sweet chocolate chips
1 cup white sugar
1 cup brown sugar
2 eggs
2 cups rolled oats
1 tsp. vanilla
Also may add chopped walnuts

Instructions

Sift together and set aside flour, soda, salt and baking powder.
Blend together shortening and sugars. Add eggs and heat until
light and fluffy. Add flour mixture and mix well. Add vanilla
rolled oats, and chocolate chips and nuts.
Drop by spoonfuls on greased baking sheet and bake 325 degrees
until brown. May also press cookies down with fork before
baking. Makes a large batch.

CUP CAKES

Ingredients

1 cup miracle whip
1 cup sugar
1 tsp. vanilla
2 ¼ cup sifted cake flour
½ cup cocoa
1 tsp. baking powder
    Dash salt
1 tsp. baking soda
¾ cup cold water

Instructions

Combine miracle whip and sugar add vanilla flour, cocoa, soda, baking powder and salt together, and add alternatively with water to miracle whip mixture. Bake at 350 degrees about 20-25 minutes for cup cakes. Makes 18 to 20.

For cake pour into waxed paper lined 8 inch layer pans and bake 350 degrees for 25-30 minutes. Make desired frosting.

PEANUT BUTTER CHOCOLATE CHIP COOKIES

Ingredients
½ cup shortening
½ cup peanut butter
½ cup white sugar
½ cup brown sugar
1 cup flour
1 egg
½ tsp. baking powder
¼ tsp. baking soda
½ tsp. salt
½ pkg. semi sweet chocolate pieces

Instructions
Cream together shortening and peanut butter. Add sugars continue creaming. Add egg and bet well. Sift together dry ingredients and blend into peanut butter mixture.
Stir in chocolate chips, drop by teaspoonfuls onto cookie sheet, flatten with a wet fork. Bake in 375 degrees oven for 12 to 15 minutes or until nicely brown.

GERMAN CHRISTMAS COOKIES

Ingredients
2 cups sugar
4 large eggs
1 tsp. ground nutmeg
1 tsp. cloves
1 tbsp. cinnamon
4 cups flour
1 tsp. baking powder
3 oz. citron peel grated
   Rind of 1 lemon

Instructions
Beat eggs and sugar together, then sift in spices, baking powder and flour. Add citron peel chopped fine and grated lemon rind. Mix thoroughly and form into small balls. Place on greased cookie sheet about 1 inch apart. Bake in 375 degrees oven for 10-13 minutes, light brown.

HONEY COOKIES

Ingredients

1 cup butter
2 eggs
1 cup brown sugar
½ cup honey melted
4 cups flour
2 tsp. soda
1 tsp. vanilla

Instructions

Mix ingredients. Roll out. Bake on greases pan 350 degrees or until done. Sandwich cookies together with jam or icing.

SHORTBREAD

Ingredients

1 cup butter (½ lb.)
½ cup brown sugar
1 egg yolk
1 tsp. vanilla
2 cups sifted flour
1 tsp. baking soda

Instructions

Cream butter, add sugar and blend thoroughly, add egg yolk and
vanilla. Sift flour with baking soda and mix well with first mixture.
Spread in ungreased pan. Prick deeply with fork. Bake in
moderate oven 350 degrees for 25 minutes.

DATE COOKIES

<u>Ingredients</u>
3 eggs beaten
1 ½ cups sugar
1 cup butter
1 tsp. vanilla
1 tsp. soda
1 tsp. cloves
3 cups flour
1 lb. Finely chopped dates (cut with scissors dipped into ht water)

<u>Instructions</u>
Cream butter and sugar, add beaten eggs and vanilla. Sift dry ingredients and add to first mixture and lastly the chopped dates. Roll out thin as possible and cut with cookie cutter or roll in balls and press out thin with bottom of tumbler dipped into hot water. Bake 375 degrees for 10-12 minutes. Makes approximately 6 dozen cookies.

MACAROONS DE LUSCE

Ingredients
4 large egg whites
13/4 cups sugar
2 cups Quick Quaker Oats
1 cup of desiccated coconut
¼ tsp. baking powder
Walnut halves for decoration

Instructions
Beat egg whites till peaks form. Add next four ingredients mixing them together gently. Spoon mixture onto baking sheets.
Top each one with one half walnut. Place sheets in 250 degree oven to dry out slowly. Macaroons should be left till firm but not hard.

PINEAPPLE NUT COOKIES

Ingredients
Sift together:
3 ½ cups flour
1 tsp. baking soda
½ tsp. salt

Cream:
1 cup shortening
1 cup sugar
1 cup brown sugar

Instructions
Add 1 (9 oz.) crushed pineapple. 1 tsp. vanilla, 2 eggs beaten, 1 cup chopped walnuts and dry ingredients. Blend well. Drop on greased sheet. Bake at 350 degrees.

FUDGE CUTS

Ingredients

2 sq. bitter chocolate
½ cup shortening
1 cup granulated sugar
2 eggs
½ cup flour
¼ tsp. salt
1 tsp. vanilla
½ cup chopped nuts

Instructions

Melt chocolate and shortening in double boiler. Remove from heat, beat in sugar, eggs, and add flour and salt. Blend well, add vanilla. Pour into greased and floured tin sprinkle with nut. Bake at 350 degrees for 30 minutes.

BUTTERSCOTCH COOKIES

Ingredients
1 cup butter
¾ cup brown sugar
1 egg yolk
2 cups flour

Instructions
Roll into ball, flatten with cookie press. Bake at 350 degrees till light brown 5-8 minutes.

PUFFED WHEAT COOKIES

Ingredients
½ cup of margarine
1 cup of brown sugar (lightly packed)
1 tsp. vanilla
1 egg
½ tsp. baking soda
1/8 tsp. salt
1 cup of flour
2 cups of puffed wheat

Instructions

Cream together margarine, sugar and vanilla, add beaten egg, mix and sift together flour, salt, soda and add to first mixture. Add puffed wheat. Drop from spoon on greased baking sheet. Bake in moderate oven 350 degrees for 15 minutes or until light brown.

MAPLE FUDGE

Ingredients
3 cups light brown sugar
1 cup rich milk

Instructions
Cover and heat to boil. Boil for three minutes. Remove cover and add 1/6 tsp. salt and cook at moderate speed with occasional stirring until mixture will form a small ball in cold water or 328 degrees with a candy thermometer. Remove from stove, add 2 tbsp. butter and ¾ tsp. vanilla. Cool, then beat until it thickens. Add walnuts or coconut and beat until thick and creamy. Then pour into buttered pan and mark into squares. 9 x 9 inch pan.

CHOCOLATE CHEESE COOKIES

Ingredients
½ cup wheat germ
1 cup soy powder
3 ¼ tsp. granulated sugar substitute
1 tbsp. breakfast cocoa (not instant)
1 cup non-instant skim milk powder
½ cup raisins
1 cup skim milk cottage cheese
3 eggs
2 tbsp. vegetable oil
3 tbsp. honey

Instructions
Mix wheat germ, soy powder, sugar substitute, cocoa, skim milk powder and raisins in a large bowl. Add cottage cheese, eggs oil and honey, blending well.
Drop 32 small mounds on oiled cookie sheet and bake at 350 degrees for about 10 minutes in a preheated oven. Makes 32 cookies.

DADS COCONUT COOKIES

Ingredients
2 cups brown sugar
1 cup butter
2 eggs
1 tsp. vanilla
1 cup coconut (desiccated)
2 cups flour
2 cups oatmeal
1 tsp. baking soda
½ tsp. salt

Instructions
Mix all ingredients together and roll in small balls. Press down
with a fork. Bake at 350 degrees for 10 or 12 minutes.
A few chopped nuts may also be added.

Pies

PECAN PIE

Crust pies:

<u>Ingredients</u>
1 cup boiling water
1 lb. lard
6 cups flour
2 tsp. salt
2 tsp. baking powder

<u>Instructions</u>
Melt lard in one cup boiling water, add flour, salt and baking powder. Form into ball let sit in refrigerator. Break off pieces as needed and bring to room temp. Before rolling. Makes 5-2 crust pies.

Pecan pie:

<u>Ingredients</u>
3 eggs
½ cup of gram sugar
1 cup pecan nuts
1 cup corn syrup
1 tsp. vanilla
½ tsp. salt
8 inches unbaked pie shell

<u>Instructions</u>
Beat eggs slightly, add sugar, pecans, corn syrup, vanilla and salt. Mix well and pour into unbaked shell. Bake in moderately slow oven of 325 degrees for 40-50 minutes. The pecans will float to top, forming a firm crust which browns nicely if cooked slowly.

GRASSHOPPER PIE

Crust:
Mix 1 ¼ cups chocolate wafer crumbs and 4 tbsp. melted butter.
Press into 9 inch pie plate and chill.

Filling:
Combine 25 large marshmallows or 3 cups miniatures.
¼ cup milk
¼ cup whipping cream

Instructions
Heat till partially melted. Then remove from heat and stir till all
melted. Cool till slightly thick. whip remaining ½ pint cream till
stiff. Fold cream, 3 tbsp. cream de menthe and 1 drop green food
coloring into marshmallow mixture. Garnish to taste.

RHUBARB & STRAWBERRY PIE

Ingredients
1 egg
1 ½ cups white sugar
    Red food colouring
3 cups cut up rhubarb
4 soda biscuits

Instructions
Line pie plate with pastry, crumble up 4 soda crackers over crust.
In a separate bowl, beat egg and add sugar and a bit of red food
colouring and beat until nice and fluffy. Add your rhubarb and
mix well. Add strawberries lastly, or if using fresh strawberries
just put a few over top of filling when putting in the bottom
crust, so they don't get mushed up. If using frozen rhubarb and
strawberries add both at the same time and put into bottom crust
and cover with top crust. Brush top crust with cream or beat up
egg, sprinkle with sugar. Bake in 450 degree oven for 10 or 15
minutes then reduce heat to 375 degrees until nicely browned and
done.

Squares

TROPICAL PEANUT SQUARES

Ingredients
½ cup corn syrup
½ cup peanut butter
1 cup flaked coconut
½ cup brown sugar
3 cups oven toasted rice cereal

Instructions
Measure corn syrup and sugar into large saucepan. Cook over medium heat, stirring constantly until sugar is dissolved and mixture bubbles. Remove from heat. Stir in peanut butter. Add oven toasted rice cereal and coconut. Stir until well coated. With back of spoon, press mixture evenly and firmly into buttered 8x8x2 inch pan. Let stand until cool. Cut into squares. Yield – 36 squares.

NANAIMO BARS

Ingredients
1 egg well beaten
1 cup brown sugar
½ cup butter
1/3 cup milk

Instructions
Bring the above to a boil and stir. Remove from stove and add 1 cup graham wafers, ½ cup walnuts, 1 cup coconut. Press mixture into pan lined with graham wafers, then put a layer of graham wafers on top. Icing on top. 1/4 cup butter, 2 tbsp. vanilla custard, 3 tbsp. milk, blend in 2 cups icing sugar.

CHERRY TORTE

Ingredients

1 ¼ cup crushed graham wafers

1/3 cup margarine

Instructions

Combine and press into 8x8 inch cake pan. Chill.

Blend 1 cup cottage cheese 2% in blender till smooth. Combine with 2 well beaten eggs, ½ cup sugar, vanilla and pinch of salt. Spread over crumb mixture. Bake at 350 degrees for 15 minutes. Top with 1 can (15-20 oz.) of cherry pie filling. Chill.

MUD HEN BARS

Ingredients
½ cup shortening (part butter)
1 cup sugar, 1 whole egg
2 eggs separated
2 cups flour
¼ tsp. salt
1 cup chopped nuts
1 cup miniature marshmallows
1 cup light brown sugar
½ cup semi sweet chocolate pieces

Instructions
Preheat oven to 350 degrees. Cream shortening and sugar, beat in 1 whole egg and 2 egg yolks. Sift flour baking powder, and salt together. Combine the two mixtures, blend thoroughly and spread batter in 9x13 inch pan. Sprinkle nuts and chocolate pieces and marshmallows over batter. Beat egg whites till stiff, fold in brown sugar. Spread over top of cake. Bake for 30 to 40 minutes, cut into bars. Makes 32 bars.

PINEAPPLE SQUARES

Ingredients

1 lb. of Crisco

6 cups flour

1 cup milk

  Salt

Filling:

1 20 oz. tin of crushed pineapple

5 tbsp. minute tapioca

1 cup white sugar

Let stand for at least 30 minutes

Instructions

Line 15x10 inch cookie sheet with pastry. Add filling and top crust. Pinch top crust with fork. Cook for 20 minutes, then pinch again with fork to let out steam. Bake at 350 degrees for 1 hour or until a light golden colour, let cool. Spread with frosting of ¼ lb. package Philadelphia cream cheese, 1 ½ cups of icing sugar, 2 tbsp. milk.

APPLE CRISP

Ingredients
6 medium size apples
¼ cup white sugar
      Cinnamon
¼ cup butter
½ cup flour
¾ cup brown sugar

Instructions
Peel apples and slice into buttered baking dish. Sprinkle with white sugar and cinnamon. Combine butter, flour and brown sugar.
Spread on top of apples. Bake 30 minutes in moderate oven 350 degrees until apples are soft and top in brown. Serves 6.

Drinks

PUNCH

<u>Ingredients</u>

1 26 oz. brandy
1 26 oz. soda water
2 25 oz. crackling rose
2 6 oz. tins frozen pink lemonade

<u>Instructions</u>

Add ice cubes to suit. Red and green cherries, orange slices may be added. This punch is served from a large punch bowl. Serves 30 people.

TIA MARIA

Ingredients
2 tbsp. instant coffee
1 tbsp. vanilla
2 cups brown sugar
½ cup water

Instructions
Bring all ingredients to a full boil in saucepan and cool. Add 26 oz. of plain alcohol.

CHINESE GIN

Ingredients
12 lemons
12 oranges
12 lb. sugar
12 potatoes
1 lb. seedless raisins
2 dry yeast
12 quarts water

Instructions
Cut up and squeeze lemons and oranges, throw in along with raisins. Mix sugar with 2/3 quarts of hot water. Spread yeast on two pieces toast and set on top of mixture. Let stand 2 weeks. Squeeze pulp and throw out. Let stand 1 or 2 days then bottle.